Yes, I Do

MY JOURNEY TO MARRIAGE AND THE STORY AFTER

Jenny A. Rogers

authorHOUSE®

AuthorHouse™ UK
1663 Liberty Drive
Bloomington, IN 47403 USA
www.authorhouse.co.uk
Phone: 0800.197.4150

Scriptures marked AMP are taken from the AMPLIFIED BIBLE (AMP): Scripture taken from the AMPLIFIED® BIBLE, Copyright © 1954, 1958, 1962, 1964, 1965, 1987 by the Lockman Foundation Used by Permission. (www.Lockman.org)

Scriptures marked KJV are taken from the KING JAMES VERSION (KJV): KING JAMES VERSION, public domain

Scriptures marked NIV are taken from the NEW INTERNATIONAL VERSION (NIV): Scripture taken from THE HOLY BIBLE, NEW INTERNATIONAL VERSION ®. Copyright© 1973, 1978, 1984, 2011 by Biblica, Inc.™. Used by permission of Zondervan

Published by AuthorHouse 06/11/2018

ISBN: 978-1-5462-8997-5 (sc)
ISBN: 978-1-5462-8998-2 (hc)
ISBN: 978-1-5462-8996-8 (e)

Print information available on the last page.

This book is printed on acid-free paper.

Open your mouth, judge righteously, and administer justice for the poor and the needy.

—Proverbs 31:9 (AMPC)

Nevertheless, in [the plan of] the Lord and from His point of view woman is *not* apart from and independent of man, *nor* is man aloof from and independent of woman. For as woman was made from man, even so man is also born of woman; and all [whether male or female go forth] from God [as their Author].

—1 Corinthians 11:11–12

(AMPC, emphasis added)

Amen.

CONTENTS

ACKNOWLEDGEMENTS

I am very grateful to God, my Father in heaven, who has brought me this far through it all, to be able to write this book according to His wisdom and His word and His divine perspective about marriage and family using my own experience. Lord, I love You deeply, and I wholly dedicate this book and its teachings to everything and anything that would promote Your kingdom as we patiently wait for Your return in glory.

I am enthused to also dedicate this book to my first son and seed, Ivan (God's gift). An experience like this wouldn't have been possible without him. I am more than pleased to be called your mother. I had an absolutely different experience throughout your birth and growing up. I continue to pray the Lord's covering, according to Psalm 91. I love you endlessly.

"That I may publish with the voice of thanksgiving, and tell all of thy wondrous works" (Psalm 26:7 KJV). Amen.

To the King of glory, in Psalm 24:7–10 (KJV), "Lift up your heads, O ye gates; and be ye lift up, ye everlasting doors; and the King of glory shall come in. Who is this King of glory? The LORD strong and mighty, the LORD mighty in battle. Lift up your heads, O ye gates; even lift them up, ye everlasting doors; and the King of glory shall come in. Who is this King of glory? The LORD of hosts, he is the King of glory. Selah." Amen.

INTRODUCTION

When I was a young growing lady who had just graduated from a nursing college in Ghana, life threw many choices at me. I decided to accept a proposal from my then fiancé to marry him in my next step of life and carry on with my dreams after that. Full of love and bloom, I felt independence together. The dream was building an unbreakable life together.

I was only twenty-three at the time and a truly devoted Christian. Marriage clouded my readiness to build my future. To my astonishment, and as you reading this can attest, different backgrounds, cultures, and personalities don't make a cooperation work or become successful if you don't work to understand each other.

This book is meant to bring to you the realities of marriage and marrying too early, the challenges and opposition life throws at you and how you can fully cope. It will also show you the purpose of God's marriage, according to His plan. After reading about my true-life events, I hope you will shape your life and mind to make better choices and decisions in terms of marriage and relationships.

Knowledge is power; be free to love wisely and better in God's kind of way.

The Phone Call

On a fine afternoon after speaking to Lucas, my fiancé, we broke off our relationship and our arrangement for a future marriage. I moved on quickly from this heartbreak since I would soon graduate as a midwife and would turn twenty-one by then.

The entertainment committee put up an awesome entertainment for all leavers, and I thought it a nice way to loosen up from the whirlwind of inconsistency I had

had for the past eighteen months. I jumped in the jam boat with my friend, and we enjoyed the night dancing and being entertained. Then, I went back to my room to find numerous missed calls from an unregistered contact on my phone.

My first instinct was to ignore and delete them, as I didn't know who was on the other end. However, I said to myself I needed find out who had repeatedly called me, as I had repeatedly ignored the calls previously, to put this person in his place.

Once I phoned the number, I found out who had called. It was someone called Robert on the other end. He was happy I phoned back and started to call my name and chat. I immediately said I couldn't recall him or his voice but we could talk some other time, as I had just come to meet his number of missed calls, which was bothering me now.

As a Christian, after my ordeal, I just decided to say to the Lord, "I don't like relationships and would love to get married to flee almighty fornication," which is highly tempting in daily life as a student midwife.

Interestingly, the next day, Robert phoned me again. He was confident he knew who I was, but I denied everything, totally telling him I sold foodstuffs in the market. He was adamant and kept calling to affirm the fact that he knew me and would like to meet me. This went on for a couple of months, and I finally admitted he was right but couldn't recall him in any way and wouldn't give him my contact.

As communications progressed, he mentored me on how I could best manage my time and study so I could come out on top in my upcoming licensing exams. I was the student representative of my year group and had lots of responsibilities with my team in planning and organizing the practical details and coordination among tutors, students, and external examiners to have successful end-of-college licensing exams.

Robert's concern attracted me to him without me knowing him or even seeing who he was. He always prayed with me as well. In one moment when we were talking, all I could think of was *Were my prayers just answered?* We communicated for five months till one day, Robert said he was travelling to America for the holidays to see his family and would get in touch once he was back so we could meet.

What are your thoughts now? I bet you may have unanswered questions, doubts, anger, or curiosity to know what on earth I was thinking, going on talking to a stranger for that long. You may agree with me that surely a good relationship should start in no such manner.

It will surprise you that many of us have encountered this form of communication and have formed relationships as friends or business partners in this way. But there is no way of finding out how many of them will lead to marriage—a successful or unsuccessful one.

Note that it is better not to phone back an unregistered contact. However, if you do answer and the call is not an emergency related to family, friends, marketers, or loved ones, be alert to end the call immediately.

You may talk to two people: a dream killer and a destiny helper.

CHAPTER 1

The Meeting

Let me walk you through how we finally met in person. Don't pinch yourself yet.

My exams were completed, and I was back in college to finish one month of extra clinical work as we waited for our results. It was an interesting time of our lives as graduates since we were asked to work due to our own silliness as students. We enjoyed each other's company and got to know ourselves much better in that time than during the entire three years we spent in training. Freshers were joining the college, and it was absolutely fun for us to be there to mentor them and share our experience.

Church attendance and religion were in full play in my life, and my slogan was "Enjoyment is good." I had fun by going to the beach, visiting live bands, and travelling within Ghana. I had lots of family members and enjoyed doing round trips as well as selling my perfumes.

One early morning, just as I was getting ready for work, my phone rang whilst I was putting on my new Diesel perfume. It was Robert. My perfume dropped from my hand and smashed to pieces in my room. I was happy to hear from him but truly had mixed emotions from the breakage of my most cherished perfume at the time. In the Ghanaian belief, this meant a bad omen. But I was sadder to lose the perfume than to think something bad would happen.

Robert was an excellent communicator and made it plain to me he loved me and wanted us to meet as soon as we could. He had very important things to share with me. I still wondered what all this was about, but my inner curiosity wanted to find out who this confident man on the other side of the phone was.

Finally, the day came to meet. He requested I make him his favourite dish and meet him in a hotel. As a young Christian, I didn't think this the ideal path to follow, as it was plain temptation would follow. But all my claws had come out to feel the full splendour of what would happen when I saw him. So I did as he wished.

On that evening he arrived at my campus, it began raining like cats and dogs, and I just had to go with him to his hotel as we discussed on the phone. He was a dark, tall, and muscular man. He looked more fearful than handsome. He was full of laughter and smiles when we met, but inside, I was 100 per cent terrified.

I wanted to find out more about him, but it never became the case on our night out. It turned out exactly like the wild card experience that may be playing out in your mind as you read. As a sexually inactive person, I found the whole sexual experience very painful.

I saw him off the next day at the coach station and went to my home in town to reflect on what had happened to me. I couldn't believe it. What was happening to me?

You must think now, *That girl! You are no Christian. And of course how foolish, because anything could have happened to you out there.* Yes! That's so real! Let's just consider what you would do or how you would advise anyone who falls into such a trap or temptation to respond.

> "For we have not an high priest which cannot be touched with the feeling of our infirmities; but was in all points tempted like as we are, yet without sin."
>
> —Hebrews 4:15 (KJV)

CHAPTER 2

The Travel

Are you now thinking about something you skipped on a recent date or what really happened after a meeting?

Well, back to my story, we were all to complete our posting forms as the clinical practice came to an end. Robert was always on my mind, and I, the head of my midwifery class, had mistakenly completed my forms with his number as my contact.

At this time, our relationship had kicked off, and it was mainly a distant one. Telephone communication was our only tool. Robert told me he worked with the secret service in Ghana and lived in the capital, Accra, with some workmates in a flat. It was also interesting to know that he drove a silver car, as he described it, and was living very comfortably.

Well, to his amazement, I arranged with one of my relatives to spend my one-month holiday with him in Accra. My move surprised him, and we arranged to spend the first three days in his home before I finally settled in with my family.

I arrived in Accra in early February, and love was in the air. The almighty Valentine's Day was fast approaching. My sister, whom I lived with in my home city, had nothing to worry about because she totally believed I would be in our relatives' home as soon as I arrived in Accra. I completely lied and was now waiting for Robert, who had directed me to arrive in a suburb of Accra. He was very late.

It really confused me as to why I was in a suburb of the city rather than the city itself. Trust me—I know I was really naive. Basically, I was a good girl turned bad. It was definitely getting interesting. What a mystery I was facing now. I could only say, "Lord, save me and deliver me from this bad-girl behaviour."

Finally, Robert showed up in a white car with a friend driving and him in the front passenger seat. They picked me up and took me to a very old-style home. I was very shy at seeing him but did ask, "Why are we here?" It was very different from what he initially said. He said to me it was his grandmother's house, and for our privacy, he had chosen for us to go here for the weekend. That really baffled me, but I was already here, in a home that had tattered shared toilets and baths, without a kitchen.

I wondered how I would survive the next three days. I had been trained at home not to be selective and to adapt to all situations. So I adjusted throughout my stay, knowing the accommodations weren't preferable to me.

I wasn't happy with how this turned out. It greatly disappointed me, and I definitely wanted to go to my relatives' home. I met his sister, who called him by a different name, so I became greatly confused. I realized

I had put myself in a trap and thought, *What will be my escape?* I was thinking, *Hmm.*

Robert tried to convince me about his love for me and how he had purposely been in my school three times just to get hold of me. He said I was his dream wife and he would do anything to settle down with me. I couldn't say it was the same with me, but we laughed and shared our stories and hopes about life. It was time to remove the mask of lies we had both put up in this long-distance relationship.

Finally, I arrived at my relatives' home in Accra, and to them, it seemed I had just arrived from my home city. My relatives and I spoke at length, and they were proud of me and anxiously waiting with me on the outcome of my licensing exams. Robert kept communicating and occasionally paid me visits in my home whilst on holidays, and he wanted to meet my family. I told one relative about meeting this guy in the past year, and he seemed to be very much interested and wanted to meet him too.

My family was more than happy but deeply advised me on making good decisions in regards to marriage, as it may not always be as I saw it at that time. My relative and Robert met briefly and chatted. My relative wanted to know why Robert wanted to be with me, as we had a huge age gap of ten years. After their chat, my family noticed my naivety of the whole idea about settling down.

As my time in Accra passed, my dear mum told me someone close to the family, Paul, would be coming to Ghana from Europe to pick up his kids and she would love it if I travelled abroad. I wasn't happy about the news. I had a lot of relatives abroad, and I wasn't ready to go through such a hard life, which included struggling to settle due to immigration laws. I felt very comfortable and didn't want to compromise my life at that stage.

My mum has always been my close friend and knows everything about me. She wanted the best for me at all costs, but this time, her decision was something I couldn't agree to. She got Robert and one of my sisters to convince me to give travelling abroad a try.

Robert was very helpful and supportive at the time. He connected me to one of his friends at the embassy who supported me in completing all my forms and did the whole application for a visa. During these times, I travelled up and down between cities, not allowing people to know what my plans were. I mostly spent the days with Robert. Now, regardless of the deception, confusion, and mystery, I decided to let it go and give our relationship a shot due to his true commitment and support.

A week after Paul arrived in Ghana, my visa was granted. We then departed to Europe with his children. It was hard to determine the balance as to whether I was coming back or this relationship still stood. Robert strongly insisted before my departure that we go back to our telephone tool. He still wanted the relationship and dreamed of our marriage being in the near future. I hadn't met most of Robert's family, but he had met a few of my family members and spoken to some.

I travelled to Europe, not really having decided about my relationship with Robert, as I was still a very young woman. But I now saw a totally different Robert since when I had arrived in Europe. He was communicating with me daily and was very supportive financially and emotionally throughout my stay.

CHAPTER 3

The Distance

Wow! Has she lost her mind, believing he'll wait for her even though she doesn't know her opportunities abroad? I can hear you screaming; this can't be real, can it? Well, of course, it's real. You are reading about true-life events. Just before you conclude, let's dive into how the relationship progressed when I travelled.

The journey was really exciting and relaxing. I was taken aback by the beautiful and neat surroundings of the whole country. I also found it unbelievable that it was very sunny but very cold to me. Paul couldn't help but laugh and said this was summer, the warmest weather at 17 degrees Celsius. As soon as I got off my flight, my phone's roaming service activated, and I received a text from Robert expressing how much he missed me already and he meant everything he said.

As we kept texting each other on the way to Paul's home, which was outside the city, Paul became curious as to who I was texting with, and I spoke to him about Robert and his intentions. He wasn't really interested and drove along, showing me around the country on the way to his home.

Robert was always on the other end of the phone, and we talked a lot about the new environment. He also shared with me his travel experiences, which couldn't be proven true at this time. He advised I make inquiries to join the army abroad, as he knew people who joined and it would be very good to have as a career.

I told Paul, and he was happy to help me go through the process and went with me to the army careers office in the city centre, where we lived. The army staff were very nice and welcoming and handed out some leaflets on how to join them. I was very happy and shared the news with Robert. On a daily basis, we spoke about the day's experience, and now, I was convinced I was in love with him.

I told Paul everything about Robert and how I had agreed to marry him once I returned home before I joined the army as a full career. He still wasn't convinced; he thought it wasn't about time I settled down, as I had just finished college and did not have a lot of experience with life, in his opinion.

I was staying with Paul on a visitor's visa, so I couldn't work. It is believed in my native country that you are able to work abroad once you visit Europe regardless of your visa or age. Paul was very happy to provide me with food and shelter, but anything aside from that was really hard to get, and being a woman made the stay extra hard, in terms of sanitary pads and clothes.

Robert was very supportive and would send me money on a monthly basis for my upkeep if I needed something.

He also provided money to buy our wedding stuff when I returned. I got myself a voluntary job for three months but couldn't hold it down any longer due to transportation costs.

I looked after Paul's children, whom I totally loved to bits, all during my visit, till they both entered full-time school. Once they started schooling, the need for my presence in Paul's home waned, and I wasn't treated with much support in my next step. In one of our regular chats, I expressed to Robert how fed up I was now with living in the country without work. It was getting very boring, and Paul didn't support all other means to work.

Paul's wife took this chat the wrong way, and therefore, my stay had to end sooner than expected. The army extended my visa, and as soon as I received it, I made my way back home to Ghana, where Robert and I would get married before my return to Europe to begin my career in the army.

Hopefully, this had not been a complete waste of money and opportunities.

CHAPTER 4

The Return

On my arrival at Kotoka International Airport in Accra, Ghana, Robert warmly welcomed me. It had been eight months since we last saw each other, although we had kept communicating throughout my stay in Europe. Seeing him felt like our first meeting; we were both over each other. We went to his home, where I spent three days with him and was pampered to help me recover from my long round trip back to Ghana.

We did a lot of chatting, and he was happy to receive his presents and also to know I had bought most of our wedding items. Robert informed me he was now working with a station as an officer and no longer working with the secret service, so he permanently stayed in his apartment at his grandma's. The home was now transformed on my arrival, and I was really impressed by the good work he had done here. He couldn't express to me how excited he was to have me back and be together forever.

On my return, I was broke and had no money, but Robert kept on supporting me with funds to help me travel to other parts of the country to visit family and finally settle in my home city to work. I finally met my mum and other extended family members, who all told me how excited they already were about the news they had heard about my impending marriage. (Aren't you surprised, knowing I only discussed this with one family member and everyone knew already?)

On my paternal side, we are a very big business-inherited family, and quarterly meetings are held yearly. Fortunately or unfortunately for me, I arrived for the last one in the year. I had already made a few enemies with my siblings for not personally telling some of them I was travelling. Imagine having twenty or more siblings besides yourself in your paternal family. Where do you start with telling everyone your travel plans? It sounds impossible, *doesn't it*? It surely is impossible, as they are all around the globe. However, trust me; if one family member knows, everyone knows. This is true in my family. Have you spotted the trends in how your family communicates or shares information? Do so!

Also, the fact that I was the youngest and I had the travel experience didn't settle well with some of the elder ones. My trip to Europe was sponsored mainly by my dad's business, which was really supportive in my trip and extending my visa.

Just before the meeting, one family member hinted to me that all of them were not happy about the news that I had returned and would soon be married. And due to Robert's job and status, they couldn't agree, as people who had practically raised me since we lost our dad, to endorse our marriage. I was devastated but already home and couldn't excuse myself from the meeting.

Nothing new popped up after accounts were read, and I was the next on the agenda—just me. By my native culture, explaining myself to adults wouldn't work, and very nasty stuff was said about Robert, with only one sibling telling the others to stop embarrassing me till they had all met him.

I have twenty siblings, and in my mind, we only meet four times a year, so how, then, would Robert and I be able to meet all of them? I told Robert that night how my family wanted to meet him and he should react nicely to all of them, no matter on what grounds he was received. Robert had been widely introduced and accepted on my maternal side, but the story was absolutely different now for him on the paternal side.

I went back to my home city once the meeting was finished to start work. My relative there was happy to welcome me home and told me what she already knew in regards to my news. She assured me she was ready to support me and meet up with Robert and make our home his home. Robert and I kept communicating, and he was delighted he would soon meet my family.

CHAPTER 5

The Marriage

The union between a man and a woman as ordained by God is known as marriage. This union is portrayed throughout the Bible and has come along with commandments as to how human beings can procreate.

A marriage bed, as the Bible says, should be undefiled. Adultery is one of the commandments of God given to Moses. A successful marriage is defined by excellent communication, understanding, and unending sacrifice (love) and commitments for each other.

The Bible has perfectly classified that it is not good for either man or woman to live alone, for two are definitely better than one. It also clearly spells out in different parables how two can conquer life to live victoriously. It is said locally that "behind a successful man is a woman—not any woman per se, but a successful, self-sacrificing woman."

In the concept of marriage, lest we forget, the church is the bride of Christ, our coming King. Due to this, we are always in communion with Him by prayer and the last supper. As Christ expects from the church, so does He expect us to commit, love, pray, and be in relationship throughout our married lives.

In the next pages, you will find out real-life issues that throw to you the challenges of marrying and staying married and also overcoming brokenness.

God hates divorce. Per Malachi 2:16 (AMP), "'For I hate [a] divorce,'" says the Lord, the God of Israel, "'and him who covers his garment with wrong *and* violence,'" says the Lord of hosts. "'Therefore keep watch on your spirit, so that you do not deal treacherously [with your wife].'"

The Preparation

Back to my ever-dreaming home sweet home in Ghana. It was very exciting to me. Within two weeks of my arrival, I was already back at work to complete my national service program. This was also well needed to finally complete my application with the army.

I had now settled into fully working as an intern midwife. Robert and I kept communicating by phone, and he had already made plans to come regularly to visit me from Accra in my city regardless of the distance. Every effort of care and love made a big impression on me. I lost my dad at age thirteen and had since been living with my siblings, and it had been survival of the fittest.

I couldn't keep up our regular communications due to my work schedules, and it really frustrated Robert. I explained to him how I had put in all my work so as to alleviate my mind of all the negative experiences I had abroad in Europe. Robert quickly understood, and we settled on communicating with each other during breaks or after work.

It was time for Robert to finally meet my paternal siblings, beginning with my relatives I lived with. They were more than excited to meet him and know from both of us why we wanted to settle down with such a big age difference. I was very scared about Robert meeting my paternal side of the family because they had plainly said to me they didn't like his career. He was poor and certainly a gold digger. It was very awful to hear, as nobody knows tomorrow or anyone's destiny. Stars are only seen at night, when they shine in the dark and the night is still.

My relatives met Robert and welcomed him perfectly, like we were trained to do. The conversation and reception were great, and we put our marriage plans before them but was told, as a large family, we needed to meet the rest of the members as well for approval. Robert left unsettled with his plans and dreams for us. I couldn't do more than reassure him he would soon meet all of them, since we would soon get back to our quarterly meeting.

My relative advised I pray one on one with a pastor for guidance, counselling, and prayers. As it stood, my paternal side was not at all interested in the marriage. Robert met most of them on our visit to my birth city, but he wasn't welcomed.

All odds of acceptance failed on my paternal side, but my maternal side and a few members of my paternal side were all right and gave us the blessing to go ahead. In preparing, we told our plans to my church in my home city, but the bishop also refused to join us in matrimony, explaining I wasn't a permanent member of his assembly although I attended regularly and paid all tithes when I was in college.

Each step was very frustrating and confusing. I kept praying, also with the referred pastor, and encouraged Robert to pray as well. And he assured me he did, as he was always in church, and said he was part of the church protocol team. To proceed with the wedding plans, we went to my registered church in my birth city, and we were readily accepted. However, we were told a three months' prayer would be said in regards to the marriage, and once the church was happy with a confirmation, it would proceed us through to counselling, which would go on for six months.

I couldn't believe my ears, as I already had plans to begin work and university abroad. I found the delay tactic and how things had slowed down from our original plan unbelievable. Robert wanted to have a wedding, so we decided to wait and go through the process so long as I still had some months to travel.

Most of the shopping items were bought abroad; everything left in the wedding preparations had to do with custom Ghanaian marriage preparations. We happily shopped together by help of a list provided by my maternal uncle and mum. For the wedding, we needed decorations and hall hire, and supporting relatives and I sorted food.

Robert and I fully funded our marriage preparations. Ninety per cent of my paternal siblings totally backed off during that time. About a month until the ceremony, I had a series of dreams. Twice, I dreamed that all guests, family, and friends coming to my wedding ceremony were in black. A receptionist also had the same dream in my dad's company.

The pastor couldn't explain the meaning of this dream but urged us to keep praying against any skims of the devil. I personally interpreted it to mean loved ones would have an accident as they travelled on the day of the ceremony, so we ensured our guests arrived a day before the ceremony and they were warmly hosted for three nights in my dad's hotel in my birth city.

Ensure you have grown or matured enough to take this next big step: marriage.

The Ceremony

Robert's family arrived in my home for both Ghanaian custom marriage and white wedding ceremonies. They came from the Ashanti part of Ghana, whilst mine came from the Central part. By this time, most of my paternal siblings knew they had lost the battle of separating us.

They had no choice but to fully pamper and warmly welcome Robert's family, which they did perfectly.

Our custom marriage ceremony was held on a bright, sunny day. It was very lovely, beautiful, and rich. Guests, friends, and family arrived from different parts of the country to support us. The love, joy, and laughter of the day were enormous, and the food was extremely good. I couldn't help but enjoy the day as it went along. However, awkward things happened when I was finally welcomed into the middle of the ceremony, as our custom demands. I immediately noticed that the rites were performed not by my paternal family but rather by the maternal side. This was very weird, as Akan tradition doesn't allow maternal family to conduct marriage rites even in the absence of a dad; a family linguist always performs the rites. Also, days after the ceremony, we realized the dad's gift was exchanged for the mum's. I couldn't understand why such a mistake was done.

After our custom marriage ceremony, I went on to the hairdresser, who was a very close family friend of ours, to have my hair done for the wedding the next day. She was very happy to have my hair done, and we chatted a lot about how we met and why the big age difference didn't bother me and how I felt rejected due to my paternal family's attitude throughout the whole program. She reassured me and asked me if I knew anything about one of my sisters' partners. I said of course not. She began to tell me how she had just described my soon-to-be husband as her fiancé. She saw the shock on my face and immediately apologized and said she had probably heard it all wrong.

The morning of the wedding, which was the next day after the custom marriage, arrived. Robert and I communicated by phone since we were in different rooms of the same house. We were both promptly on time for the wedding. My uncle on my mum's side walked me down the aisle although most of the guests hadn't arrived yet. The ceremony continued in a solemn way, and it all seemed like we were perfect for each other. When it got to the signing of the registry, we were absolutely surprised to find out a lot of friends and family were present for the program. It was truly a joyous moment, and Robert smiled. He had found his lost rib.

We proceeded to the reception afterward, and it was full of surprises Robert planned to make the ceremony fun. At some point, Robert told me not to show how happy I was, and I quickly asked why, because I was really enjoying the love for the day. He explained to me how he'd heard of the hate from my paternal side and that they weren't happy for us. The message got to me, and I couldn't fully be happy throughout the ceremony.

Our wedding was most talked about in our town after the ceremony. Robert organized his karate team to display a show of tae kwon do at the wedding, and also, his officers' team did a flash performance. This was fun and very much enjoyed by our guest. The food and cake were excellent, made by my sister, who is a head chef.

At the end, we gave nothing but thanks to our God, took photos, and went straight to our honeymoon.

CHAPTER 6

After the Vows

We arrived in our hotel room after our photo shoot with our bridesmaid and best man. We said a thank-you prayer, and I was reminded to take off my crown before 6 p.m., so I did. We were hungry and tired. Our bridal team had picked up and delivered our bags here, where we enjoyed our homemade dinner. Then, it was just the two of us when our bridal team left.

Communication didn't seem right, as Robert was entirely on his phone and spent the rest of the night calling and messaging friends to express our gratitude for their coming to our wedding. I was thinking we would both reflect on the day and plan our future, or what next to do from here. Robert fell entirely asleep later, but of course, it was our honeymoon night, so I reminded him of the fun part with a candlelit surprise of love when he woke, and we made love.

Still in a wedding bliss, we got ready for church service the next day. I had amazing makeup done, by my makeup artist who came to our hotel to help me dress up and look beautiful in my tailored Ghanaian dress. The church sermon was exquisite, and we were highly acknowledged for our dedication to each other during our counselling times. The congregation, the priest, and family and friends gave us best wishes and blessings. It was awesome.

Robert's family had been travelling for four days now, and they really loved to stay on, but I couldn't agree to that, as the cost involved was extremely high. And their accommodations were my family's business, and my family couldn't risk a day without business. I could understand my family's concerns, but Robert didn't. He also had forgotten the fact that we didn't have any more money after the wedding ceremony due to all the costs involved.

After our private deliberations, he finally understood and told his family they had to leave. My stepfather gladly dropped all of them off at the station. Robert wasn't happy that we hadn't been able to communicate properly for the past few days. I couldn't keep text messaging whilst he was there with me or in the same home.

Our plan for my return abroad was for us to get married abroad quickly in a smaller ceremony and then go back to complete my course and training. However, marriage in Ghana is seen as very solemn, and therefore due to the process, my travel plan would be delayed for up to six months. This was the day we had been waiting for, but after the ceremony, the communication and joy seemed to have died out. Robert was very attached to his phone and social media. The two of us didn't agree on anything.

The evening when his family had departed, Robert and I had a misunderstanding when sorting out our photos with the photographer. Robert wanted a smarter way out, where we had all the pictures on a pen drive and we didn't have to pay for our photos. I was shocked about this and had to foot the bill for our photos myself for the sake of love and to prevent disgrace.

All my friends knew me to be a talkative and funny, bubbly, loving person. But with Robert, I would rather leave him to do the talking and make suggestions, as I realized he was quick-tempered, and due to our age difference (ten years), he thought my ideas were too young. Within the short time, Robert had developed a profound anger in his heart and didn't explain to me what was eating him up. My apologies for if I had done anything wrong fell on deaf ears, but we still had to carry on in our marital bliss (which was a myth).

The next day, we spent most of the day showing appreciation to our family, friends, pastors, and neighbours. This was because I would soon be travelling abroad, and it would be long before we saw them again. We then embarked our journey to my home city, where I used to work and live. I was now totally relocating to live with Robert, as we were now married. Robert was still upset and not communicating because he couldn't finish drawing up a plan for one of his friends who liked one of the houses he saw in my neighbourhood. I explained and reassured Robert we could always go back to my hometown for him to complete the plan. He still wasn't happy.

On our arrival to my city, my whole family welcomed us with love and joy. A special room was prepared for us as a couple. It was a happy moment for all of us. My sister prepared Robert's favourite meal, and we enjoyed dinner together. Eventually, Robert was happy. He shared his joy with his family and friends on the phone, and I also spoke to them as well. I began to realize the true Robert as each day passed. He loved to talk about our relationship on the phone as if it were going good, but in reality, it wasn't. He basically forgot we had been in a relationship before we went to the altar to be blessed for it and nothing should change that, in our hearts, actions, or minds.

On this day in our journey, we had no money after the ceremony, so travelling from my city to Robert's city seemed impossible. Robert didn't want to accept wedding gifts of any kind, either in cash or items. But I explained to him we had to use some of the money to buy tickets to his city and also spend some till we both got paid. Robert didn't agree to this step and became more furious. I wondered what to do at that point, as he had no funds himself, and wished he would understand.

We spent the next day again showing our appreciation to my colleagues in the hospital and my matron for the numerous gifts that kept coming. They were all happy and full of smiles. I quickly had an ultrasound to confirm whether I was pregnant, as I suspected. During the counselling period, I was so unwell sometimes, and I definitely needed confirmation at that time about how far I had gone in the pregnancy. It was already sixteen weeks.

Robert had a son already but hadn't met him. He lived abroad with his mum and did not regularly stay in contact. He told me this on my return abroad, and I accepted it. He was excited about my being pregnant and wanted me to keep the baby since he realized I was unwell from counselling.

By the next morning, I had used funds from our gift to aid us in travelling back to Robert's home. He still wasn't happy, but I had no option. Once I had bought the tickets, Robert asked for the gift of money we had received, and I gave it to him submissively, but he still wasn't happy. Halfway on our journey, the photographer gave us our beautiful wedding album and framed pictures. They were so beautiful, and it cracked a smile on Robert's face, which was very heartwarming to see.

We finally got to Robert's house, which was the same house he said was his grandmother's house and his hideout. Robert had never worked with the secret service as he claimed initially and clearly didn't have a car, but I forgave him for his lies and was happy to work through them in the marriage. We were warmly welcomed by my sister-in-law, who lived in another apartment in the same building. She welcomed us with a meal and asked us about our journey and assured me to let her know if I needed anything since we now lived in the same house.

Robert quickly got on the phone to let his friends know we were now in his town and living together. Unfortunately, Robert was still angry and didn't communicate to me about why he was so. I did apologize in case I had said or done something that made him angry, but our relationship remained cold. He was happy to talk with his friends on the phone or on social media just to pretend we had a good relationship, but this was not so. It baffled me.

A successful marriage cannot be founded on lies. Be real and truthful. Love and accept your partner just the way he or she is.

Together Apart

We had now been living together for three weeks and gone to church together once. I was not working at the time because I was sorting out my transfer from work to Accra. The transfer was not successful at the time. Robert and I hadn't been recognized in his church, as was normally done to introduce a new couple to the church if they married elsewhere. We laid down all our money on the altar in his church, as insisted by Robert, even though we had no money to sustain us or our food and water. We were both now relying on our salaries at the end of the month.

We lived together but only talked sometimes. Robert was mostly at work in the day from 6 a.m. to about 8 p.m. Due to my travel plans, I was not working. As soon as Robert returned from work, I would make his shake so he could train in our home gym. He loved bodybuilding, and I liked it as well. It was always fun to see him train and be fit for his job. Also, I was always assured 100 per cent protection with him, for he was always fit and strong.

After his training session, Robert would have his dinner and go straight back to his laptop, chatting with friends on Facebook or downloading his bodybuilding videos. This would last to about 1 a.m. We barely discussed anything in regards to our future or the unborn baby. Anytime I mentioned it, he would say he was tired and we could discuss that on his off day. However, he would be on his laptop and mostly sleeping around 2 a.m. We only had the chance to share laughter together when we both saw our favourite advert on the television. Robert and I had no sexual relations again after our honeymoon night.

I couldn't understand what was going on in our marriage. Robert bought stuff for the home, provided water, and helped me hang washed clothes and even iron them, but he was still very cold towards me. I wondered why the very person who got me interested in him was now drawing away from me and the unborn baby. We quarrelled about him not communicating with me and being angry all the time, our having no sexual relations and no plans for our unborn baby in regards to our accommodations for when he was born.

Robert was furious and began cursing me, and I said to him there and then that none of his words would work. And although he said he was a Christian, none of his actions since we got married portrayed him as one. He called me a liar and pretender when I prayed. This didn't change anything between us and brought me great sorrows and tears as to who would help me if I shared this and how my family would react to this news, because they clearly didn't support this union from the very beginning.

This unfaithful lifestyle of his talking to people on the phone about a nonexistent happy marriage whilst there was no joy in the home kept me wondering. *Hm …* *what really happened before we spoke on the phone, became friends and lovers, got married, and were now expecting a baby? What about all the sacrifices we had to go through with counselling and me defying my paternal family's views to just be with him as he fully supported me whilst I was in Europe?* I bet you are wondering as I did.

Happiness left me in the marriage. Robert would quickly run from our home anytime my relatives or friends visited us. We didn't have an enclosed kitchen or a private toilet, but I wasn't shy about that because I totally believe in small beginnings. I had already contributed some funds with Robert so we could have our private one, but no action was taken on that.

At last, the day finally arrived when I had to leave. I was still torn apart from the horrible three weeks we had lived together as a couple—no communication, understanding, decisions, or sexual relations. I could only pray to God for some of these problems to be solved, as I was going away. Robert took me to the airport and apologized for what had been happening at home. He also proudly told his friends that his wife was travelling abroad with her pregnancy. Only Robert knew his reason to have married me, as I couldn't understand his pretence.

I joyfully relaxed, and off I went back to Europe with Virgin Atlantic Airlines, happy to meet my family and friends abroad and also to share with them pictures and videos of our wedding ceremony.

Disagreements and Disappointments

I arrived in Europe happy to see my friends now turned family, who lovingly received me. We had a wonderful chat about my wedding and how good and bad it was, but we came through, and we were happy for now. We enjoyed our best moments there, but Robert and I decided we would have our baby back home in Ghana due to a lack of family support abroad and immigration issues. Robert had agreed to all our plans and was ready to see us soon in Ghana after the deferral of my training and education with the army.

I would be in Europe at that time as long as my deferral would take me. My first point of contact was my army recruiter who had given me the job, including sorting out my immigration. I previously lived with Paul, but due to a change in circumstances, I had to travel back and forth to my lovely friends to get through the deferral process. I regularly encountered challenging days with the travel and distance, as I was pregnant. Some days, I thought I would have a miscarriage from the speed and bumps encountered by the train, but the Lord kept us.

My hospital appointments to prove I was pregnant (as I had a very small bump) to the army were easy to follow. Paul completely abandoned me although I went to his city to complete the process. He was only interested in when

I would go back to my friends, the moment I arrived at his home, and my return date to Ghana. This was so uncomfortable to me in my condition. He and his wife were unbelievable on their reception to me. On one of my travels to him, he completely packed all my stuff and left it in my friend's house, as he was going to my friend's city. On that day, I had to leave his home immediately after I finished my appointments, and I got back around 1 a.m., vomiting and so unwell.

My friends supported me to get better and assured me they would always be there for me and their home was always my home. Truly they lived up to it. Proverb 18:24 (NIV) says, "One who has unreliable friends soon comes to ruin, but there is a friend who sticks closer than a brother."

I always shared all my anxieties, worries, and fears, especially what I was going through with Robert. He was lovely to support me whilst I was in Europe, as previously. He called usually like never before, but this time round, he couldn't fund our baby's shopping, which surprised me. I couldn't do anything else but ask my mum to support me with funds to complete my baby shopping.

Gradually, Robert's call started fading whilst I was abroad for this short stay. He neither picked up his phone calls nor texted me or responded to my texts like usual. This was rather unusual of him because he loved to communicate by phone and on social media all the time. I got all my pregnancy scans and care abroad and gladly sent Robert a copy, which he never opened. It was very clear to see we were expecting a baby boy. It was very adorable, and I would always speak to him in my womb. It was a priceless moment to be pregnant. This was my first pregnancy.

Robert was more interested in my army recruitment than our baby and actually contributed very little or none to the welfare and plans concerning him. He never expressed to me to date his true feelings on us having a baby. He may never have wanted it from the start.

All my efforts to explain to Robert our needs for a good, healthy, and improved accommodation when we would soon come back to Ghana fell on deaf ears. He always said he was busy at work and then hung up, which clearly showed his lack of interest in me and the baby, and he also never put in any suggestions or shared his plans for us. Since I had met Robert, he hadn't been truthful, but for the sake of his help when I first travelled abroad, I decided to marry him. *Coming along this far,* I thought, *I have really made a terrible mistake.* My friend noticed I wasn't happy after my phone calls, but I couldn't open up to her at the time.

I rather was able to express my dissatisfaction with my marriage with my mentor. He advised me, if possible, to stay on and have the baby if I could afford it. But unfortunately, I couldn't, since I was not working and the friend I was living with was also pregnant. Soon enough, I got my deferral from the army by post through Paul, who had already opened and read my letter and told me prior to receiving it that the deferral had been denied and I couldn't ever reapply to the army so I should go back home to Ghana.

It was obvious Paul didn't like me at that time of his life and completely rejected me. Upon receiving the letter, I found it said otherwise. My deferral was allowed, and I could rejoin after completing breastfeeding. It made me really happy, and I was at ease and now preparing to go back home to deliver the baby.

I immediately informed Robert the process had now gone through, and I would soon return to Ghana. I was thirty-six weeks pregnant and took permission to travel from the doctor before leaving Europe. Robert didn't sound cheerful, but I couldn't even realize it because of the joy of my going back home. My sponsors had been very supportive throughout my stay, and I didn't want to overburden them with my wants and needs. I was aware of the struggles of living abroad, and I couldn't see my friend's husband suffer from two pregnant women under his roof with an older child already.

I continued to ask Robert if he had received our baby's scan I posted to him. He said yes and he loved it. The baby shopping was now complete with support from my mum, myself, friends, and some family. I was finally happy and hopeful that things would be better between us as I returned home to Ghana. I had so much to share with Robert and couldn't wait to see him and hug him and talk all night about this travel experience.

The night before I left for Ghana, I dreamed Robert and I had a heated argument; he told me to go back abroad, "I don't need you here." I woke up very sad and disturbed. As a Christian, I believed in my dreams as a message from God on my future. I quickly prayed that God would redeem us from this dream and shared it with my friend because I was quiet all day. She reassured me not to worry.

I told my friend I honestly didn't want to come back to Europe after my baby to continue my program. She smiled and told me, "Of course, you shall be back, and we are happy to receive you anytime you come back." This was because since I had first travelled outside of Ghana, my family had hated me with a passion, and everything I set to do so far hadn't been successful or achievable. Nevertheless, my life and the life of my unborn child were in the hands of God, as I believed. We drove off to the airport, and we said our byes and thank-yous.

On my arrival at Kotoka International Airport in Accra, I met Robert, who immediately told me he had not been feeling well. He had come down with severe malaria and, with the help of his friend, managed to pick me up from the airport. One of my cousins' husbands met us to pick up his parcel from me and was very happy to meet us both, because he missed our wedding.

I was very grateful to Robert's friend, who had done us this favour. I was also very tired and had jet lag; I nearly passed out in the airplane and had to be treated specially by the air hostess. I couldn't unpack my items immediately on my arrival home to give Robert's friend a gift straightaway as Robert had wanted. Robert got very upset with this and ignored me, not really welcoming me at all.

As he had already told me, he was unwell and had not yet been to the hospital; he informed me his nephew was now taking over our second room. I introduced myself and sent him to change some money into Ghanaian Cedi so Robert could have treatment immediately. I wondered why Robert had no money, because he totally refused to contribute to any shopping I did for the baby.

After relaxing for a while, I woke up to sort out all my stuff and realized six perfumes had gone missing from my stuff. I gave gifts to Robert's sister and daughter and other family members as the days passed. Robert was still furious I didn't give his friend a gift, and I explained to him to share his ones if possible, and I would make it up to him. He was unhappy and upset and ignored my suggestion.

I contributed funds previously meant for Robert to improve our kitchen and toilets whilst I was away so we could have a good and healthy environment to welcome the baby. We also discussed that if this was not done, I had to deliver the baby in my home city at my dad's house, which he and my relatives had already agreed to. To my utmost surprise, nothing was done to improve our home, and as a pregnant woman, I didn't find it convenient to be sharing, because I couldn't clean. I was due to deliver in a month's time. In our courtship, Robert and I had discussed doing this, but since he couldn't keep to his word, he kept running or leaving me alone in the home when my friends or family visited because our place of convenience wasn't conducive.

Robert's coldness persisted for days even upon my return, and our communication was the same. He occasionally called me from work to check on me and the baby. He had now begun going to only night shifts, so most nights, I was alone. This was very scary, as I informed Robert I could have the baby any minute and needed him to be around. But it fell on deaf ears; he said nothing could be done about it.

I endured that and prayed every night for God's protection. I felt neglected and no longer secure with him. I was very unhappy at that time and had no sexual relationship from our honeymoon night on. Robert stopped going to church with me and started calling me a hypocrite when

I was praying daily with tears, as I couldn't sleep most nights. He did eat my food and like how I managed the home, but he hated myself and the unborn baby to bits. He never came to my antenatal visits, and to my surprise, upon cleaning the house on one of the days, I saw a scan I posted to him from Europe on the floor, and it wasn't even opened.

I guess you yourself are in shock at what kind of marriage or relationship this was.

Broken Peace

I became quiet and started reflecting on the turn of events from the beginning of the relationship till now. On one of Robert's days at home, when he finally said he was off in a month, I said to him we needed to talk. I told him unfortunately, I wouldn't be able to have our baby in Accra, as the facilities were not in place for our child, and giving birth in my previous hospital would make the whole process very easy to me, as I was familiar with the staff. Also, my mum, who would support me after I delivered, wouldn't have a place to live as she did that. Robert didn't like the idea but didn't provide other options to make it suitable.

Robert never attended my pregnancy clinic visits with me, so I told him I had extra shopping to do and would need his support of funds, as I didn't currently work. I explained to him I needed these items for the delivery day, for which he gave me money to do the shopping, but it was quite late. On Christmas Eve, my friend and I went out to buy the items. It was quite a busy time of the year, as the next day was Christmas Day. On our return, we had an accident, where a car hit the back of my taxi/cab. I was fine, including the baby, and realized I had lost my purse in the process. We changed cabs and went home.

Three days after, on one faithful Sunday morning after cooking Robert's favourite meal and going to church, I felt severe abdominal pains, and it was excruciating. Robert had not returned from work in the morning, which was about 9 a.m. now. His night shift finished at 6 a.m., but he was still not back. I tried to get hold of him, and his phone was off. In so much pain, I immediately called one of his friends (bless him) who worked in the same office to let Robert know I was unwell and told him I was pregnant. His colleague was astonished because no one in the office knew, and they wouldn't have put him on night shift if they knew I was back in the country and pregnant.

I called my mum and immediately got hold of her. She was in Accra for the festive season and visited me several times on arrival but couldn't stay with us because we didn't have an extra room to accommodate her. My mum immediately rushed to me and told me to take a deep breath as it got more painful. I still couldn't reach Robert, so his friend finally got hold of him when he called another colleague at work that resumed in the morning and said he was found sleeping in the staffroom but was now on his way. My mum arrived first, and Robert soon afterwards. My mum is a midwife and had practised nursing for many years, so she advised we go to the nearest clinic.

I was immediately taken to a nearby clinic accompanied by all of them, including one of Robert's friends, who visited at the time. We were informed it was a false labour, so this meant I would soon deliver. We were sent back home on paracetamol; however, the pain kept escalating. I dished out the food I had already made to our visitors now at home with us and supporting us. Robert wanted me to give more to his friend even though I had given him more than enough. I told Robert I was not in better health to cook for him, and I believed his friend would be able to make do with what I had dished. This triggered Robert's anger, and he was more upset than before. I really couldn't understand him, as I was saving some for him because I wouldn't be able to cook some more later. I apologized to him for making him upset. His friend left after the meal.

Lo and behold, by evening, I couldn't bare the pain at all, so I was quickly rushed to the hospital, where I was admitted for three days accompanied by my mum and Robert. It was night, so they all left after I safely secured a bed and I had drips on. I was feeling very unwell. Foetal scans showed the baby to be super active, alive, and well, but they couldn't really determine what else was wrong with me because their checks seemed fine. My mum came to check on me daily when I was admitted, but Robert never stepped foot in the hospital. He did call to check if I was okay but said to me he didn't have the money to pay for my medication or bills. My mum paid off my bills and medication upon discharge, which was the New Year.

Robert then came to pick us up. The nurses were surprised he never visited me. but I said to them he was busy with work; that was why my mum was always there. He wasn't happy thinking I had mentioned something to the nurses, which I wouldn't do, because our health was more important to me. Once I arrived in our home, I realized my antenatal book I gave to Robert to take home had been left lying outside his sister's apartment, not our own, meaning it had been there all the time we were in the hospital. At that moment, I made up my mind this relationship and marriage wouldn't work, and therefore, it wasn't healthy to keep staying with him.

Do not compromise your beliefs or integrity for marriage.

The Baby

The holidays were now over, and my mum had returned to her city to continue with her work. Only three weeks were now left for me to deliver the baby. I began packing my things, for the baby and myself. Robert had previously agreed for me to deliver in my city due to poor environmental issues in our home. Robert had kept on with his coldness for many days since my return. He was quiet whilst he saw me packing and didn't say a word, for he had plainly said to me at that time he had no money to take me to the city and he wouldn't come to my home.

I became tired of crying daily due to neglect of communication and no sexual relations with him. It was plain to me now that there was no love between us although I had opened my heart to love and trust him. Otherwise, he had his own hidden agenda for our marriage, which he couldn't achieve.

I was now ready to leave regardless of what he said, had, or did not have. I discussed with him that since he was always "busy" at work and not available, one of my friends had agreed to take me to my home. I also further explained to him I and the baby were predisposed to risk of infection and complications if we kept living there.

On the night before the travel, he said to me he would go with me and was still cold. I said it was fine and I would let my friend know the change in plan. This time, he came to share the bed with me, which hadn't happened in months. While he was there, I opened up my heart to him and told him he had made me *regret* the vows we shared at the altar, and I regretted ever saying, "Yes, I do!" to him, and I never thought in a second or minute he would treat me this way, because I felt he hated me with passion for no wrong I had done to him he had expressed to me. I asked him, "Is this the mystery why you came into my life, that way to marry and destroy me? Bring shame, disappointment, neglect, and pain upon me?" (Imagine the bedroom now.)

Robert was quiet and couldn't say a word because I finally spoke my heart out. We both slept in our different spaces and corners. Morning came, and we woke up ready to leave. Robert apologized for all he had put me through. I was speechless and couldn't alter a word (he was forgiven). We set off after telling his family (sister and mum), who wished us well. In the bus, we were in different seats till we got to my city.

I put myself together and was very happy to see my family, who welcomed us with open arms of love and such joy. They had already prepared my room and prepared Robert's favourite dish, which we both ate. Robert then told me he was scared to make love to me because I was pregnant. I couldn't believe that but kept on being excited, as I was home now, where both I and the baby would have support when I delivered, and also my mum would have a place to live when she came along. Robert left as I settled in and, of course, said he had work the next day.

My relatives and staff at our home were just so happy to see me. I was told about my exercise regime and how they would support me. I was treated like a princess as always. Home was definitely sweet home. It was a happy moment to meet all my friends in the hospital where I used to work on my first antenatal visit there. Everything was good, and my midwife told me by next week, the baby should be due. Robert and I kept communicating by phone. It was still cold as we didn't talk about anything diverse, "How are you and the baby?" and nothing more.

I told Robert to send me some money, as the baby would be due soon. He didn't, and by the next week, I was already admitted to the hospital, ready to deliver. Although my pain was minimal, I was in labour. My relative immediately gave me financial assistance as I inquired her.

My mum hadn't arrived and said she couldn't come for the time being since her leave hadn't started. Robert didn't rush down either when I told him I was already admitted to the hospital. God bless my sister, who dealt with all the ups and downs and the payment. Though the pain started slowly, it increased by the minute. At a point, I was throwing up everything I ate. I kept throwing up everything I ate. I was sweaty, angry, and touchy, and the pain continued to increase and intensify, and finally, it was time for the delivery couch. In less than five minutes, my big baby was out. I had delivered a bouncy baby boy, very fair in complexion, very tall in height, with curly hair who looked like my mum.

I burst with joy, and all the pain I had endured felt like it never happened. I informed Robert immediately by phone, and he was extremely happy.

CHAPTER 7

The Process
(Renewing of the Mind)

Don't expect to be treated the same way you were raised in marriage.

I was discharged the same day to go home from the hospital. Both I and baby were doing very well. I was very happy and filled with so much love and tears, so glad to have my own son. It was a splendid moment and a wonderful feeling. The next day, I got help from our neighbour (an older woman) who came to care for my baby and support me. I expected Robert to call regularly to express the same joy for us having the baby boy, but he called me once a day just to check on us and hadn't arrived since I delivered. I received money from Robert after my delivery and reimbursed money back to my relative who funded the process. My mum came three days after and supported me and the baby for the next three months.

As weeks passed on after the birth, I developed complications in the second week. My son got circumcised, but Robert had still not visited us. The picture was now clear that I had entered the wrong marriage, and also, I married the wrong person. I couldn't explain it to my family, as they wanted to know if he had already come to visit his son after delivery.

Surprisingly, not only was Robert not visiting, but his whole family and some family members of mine weren't as well. It was as if all the phone calls and messages didn't get to them. God bless my sister, who was our comfort and kept advising me that the child was innocent and a blessing, although I wasn't bold enough to let her know that my world was crushing me at the moment. My mum always saw me as strong and happy till one of her friends asked her to question me about how I felt.

That day, I burst out in tears and told her all that had happened since we got married. I could see the frustration on my mum's face to hear all this news in one day. Out of respect, she didn't call Robert but kept being nice to him and told him she understood as he explained to her that work was keeping him from seeing his wife and baby. One of my relatives on the outskirts of Ghana invited me to her home together with her husband. Just before we would travel to her, I informed Robert about changing our location soon.

A month after the delivery, Robert showed up at 12.45 a.m. The baby was asleep. We had waited for him, as he had said he was coming after work. I was happy to see him and served him upon his arrival but didn't eat at the time, as it was too late. He asked how I was and took some photos of the baby. As we settled down in my room to talk, I asked him what really kept him from visiting us, because he hadn't even visited me since the last time we came together.

Robert immediately got upset, left my room, and went to stay in the lounge all night, refusing to stay with me in the bedroom. I apologized but refused to talk, so I finally went to bed alone. At 4 a.m., he came by to tell me he wanted to leave. I told him to stay so we could say thank you to my relatives and our neighbour, who had been very supportive of me since I delivered. He agreed with hesitation.

When morning broke, Robert and I met with my family and showed our appreciation to both my family and neighbours. My sister said to him I would soon be home with him but advised him to visit often, as the distance between my city and Accra, where he worked, was not too far. The road had been newly constructed, and the journey was much smoother and safer than before. The baby was bathed and still sleeping whilst Robert left at 7 a.m. for Accra.

Communication between us broke down completely after Robert's visit. He began sending me ugly texts, saying I was very ungrateful to ask him what kept him from visiting us for so long. He kept sending these messages for a week, referring me to all he did for me whilst I was abroad. I was upset and worried, as I was breastfeeding, and it really made me very emotional.

My mum assisted me in replying to him in a polite way, asking him to stop sending these texts, as I was breastfeeding, and if he made me unhappy, it could affect the child. I called his closest friend to let him know what had been going on. What he heard really shocked him because his friend always told him we were perfect and he visited me often. I told him that was not true and Robert had only visited us once after the delivery, and now, he was sending me horrible texts. His friend said he phoned him about it, and as soon as he mentioned this to Robert and he started speaking his lies about us, his friend told him, "Your wife called me," and he hung up immediately. Robert didn't answer his calls again.

Whilst preparing to spend the coming months with another relative, I told Robert to come up with a name for the child, as required by custom in Ghanaian culture. Robert texted me a name days after, I told him, but I disagreed, as it didn't seem like it would have a good impact on the future of the child. I told him he could name him after himself since I liked his name, but he said no.

A baby dedication was arranged at my local church, and the date and time were communicated to Robert. On the day of the dedication, Robert came along with his friend, and I was surprised because none of his family members—not his sister or mother—was with him. He had asked me not to inform his family earlier because he would do so himself, but on arrival, it seemed he didn't. I was greatly unhappy, and what's more, he didn't contribute anything to the refreshments of the day but took some to give to his family back in Accra. He was just unbelievable. After the dedication, he took money from me to travel back to his city (awkward, right?).

My deepest regret in life has been getting married to him, for he caused me grief, shame, and disgrace. As soon as we got married, he showed me his true colours, and I deeply bless God because he couldn't hide this for thirty years or forty years and showed it soon so I could break free and have a second chance at life.

By three months old, our son had only met his dad twice, and we relocated to the northern region of Ghana to be close to my other relatives. My family was fully supportive and loving. My relative's husband tried to speak to Robert to help build our relationship, but Robert was so arrogant and proud that he hung up on him and never picked up any of his calls.

My mentor abroad advised me it was time to come back, and therefore, plans were made for me to travel back to Europe in a hard way: to leave my son and pursue my opportunity I left behind and then come back for my son. Although it was very hard to take this initiative, looking back at the loss of my whole family, my friends, and my loved ones, and the shame and disgrace, I made the move back to Europe to continue life from where I left off before all this happened.

To the glory of God, I went through the process of renewing myself and my mind to be able to write this book. I hope the events you have read have now changed some perceptions and personal choices you have made or are about to make in regards to your future.

Life is lived once. Mistakes are inevitable, but if you do err in life, don't stay down; break free, and learn from your mistakes.

God's Marriage and Family

Marriage, also called *matrimony* or *wedlock*, is a socially or ritually recognized union between spouses that establishes rights and obligations between themselves, between them and their children, and between them and their in-laws. It is the process by which two people make their relationship public, official, and permanent. It is the joining of two people in a bond that putatively lasts until death, but in practice is increasingly cut short by divorce.

God plainly said in His Word He hates divorce. Although there are several approaches to God's kind of marriage and approach to relationships, always bear in mind these three principles.

1. **Love:** In giving His Son, God demonstrated His unconditional love to mankind. Therefore, marrying is the act of giving yourself up for love, which is immeasurable and doesn't record any wrong, as evidenced by the ever-flowing precious blood of Jesus Christ our Lord (1 Corinthians 13).

2. **Transparency:** God gives accounts of His creation and when He first created the world and everything in it. Therefore, in our relationships, He expects us to be open, speaking the truth to each other in all things (Genesis 1; John 8:32).

3. **Procreation:** Everything God created was good. Therefore, in His divine nature, He has commanded us to multiply by not only giving birth to children but also being creative and innovative (Genesis 1:28).

Dating

- Decide right and be firm on whether you definitely want to meet this other person before going out on a date.

- Dress simply and uniquely, and be yourself.

- Dating means going out with someone to find out who he or she is. It doesn't affirm love in the beginning. Lust can be its start, but dating can turn out differently if it starts with just getting to know each other and becoming friends.

- List your expectations and who and what you are interested in. It saves you time and prevents you from making costly mistakes in life like I did. Nobody knows each other before marriage or any relationship.

- There will always be a starting moment where you meet somebody. It can happen by any means of communication, such as through a face-to-face talk, through a friend's or family member's introduction, online (Facebook, Twitter, LinkedIn, Instagram, a dating site, and so on), or by phone.

- Meet at a public place where you two can be seen together—a nice place to get to know each other from the start, a place of experience where you both can chat longer and find out about your religious status, work, likes and dislikes, skills and activities, hobbies, dreams and life ambitions, family, and friends.

Most first dates will honestly provide these answers and tell you if he or she wants to date you again.

- Don't cook on your first date! You are not yet married.

- Don't have sex on a first date, and better yet, stay celibate till marriage. Respect, unity, and trust build between you two as you wait. Love then grows stronger and better between the two of you.

- Look out for rigging points of nature and friends as you begin the relationship. If you have mysteries or unanswered questions around your dates, your relationship will have a 90 per cent chance of going wrong, with one person getting hurt or disappointed in the end about pretences and lies. When you build approval around you and a peace settles within you, that is a good sign that your relationship has a 60 per cent chance of success.

Take it slow, and decide if he or she is for you.

Forming Relationships

- Friendship is the key to any relationship. Many a times, our hearts make a decision faster than our minds. Therefore, take a break from the inflow of emotions that floods your heart, and think about all the conversations you have had from your first date till now and reflect. If all you have discussed matches your emotions, you have met your dream man or woman.

- Everyone wants to be with the best—someone they can be proud of regardless of the match—and this most times leads to a lot of lies and deception. Avoid lying, and *be real* from the beginning of any relationship, be it a friend, love, or business relationship.

- Be confident to speak about your relationship from the beginning with your family and closest friends. Once there is nothing to hide, *be open*. Every dark and hidden thing is a *mystery*, and you will spend days, months, and years uncovering it once you are bonded together, and it will not be as easy to come out as it was to enter.

- Time to think things over shouldn't be missed. Make decisions with the heart and mind. Be cautious to create time for every step you want to take in moving forward in any type of relationship, be it love or business.

Dealing with Family in Relationships

- Only give information that you are sure of. As soon as one family member knows something, the whole family will know it despite your readiness or lack of it.

- Make your relationship stage and message clear to prevent any form of confusion or conflicts.

- Know the difference between a family relationship and a love relationship. *Don't confuse the two.* Love comes in different forms, and you may not be able to choose.

- Keep family matters as family matters. What you say in love can be used to hurt you later in love when it has progressed to marriage. This may not always come to pass, as it depends on individual characters and personalities.

Family relationships will always be mended. Blood will always be thicker than water.

Must-Knows

- Love overrides all odds (1 Corinthians 13:4–8).

- The rich prefer to always marry the rich. This is because they believe it makes them more powerful and gives them a common interest. Relationships of opposing circumstances, such as rich–poor relationships, marriages, or businesses, are very rare. This is also due to the fact that it may not be possible for people to think equally if your interests widely differ. If such a relationship or marriage occurs, you will have to live daily to defend your position or status in that marriage or relationship. (This point is debatable.)

- The voice of the people is the voice of God. In deciding, agree to disagree.

- Money or financial support can't buy any form of acceptance in one's family. You *cannot* afford to be in any relationship just due to merits or benefits.

Before the Wedding

- Pray by yourself until you hear the voice of God, depending on your beliefs and spirituality.

- Have a clear meaning unto every revelation or dream concerning your marriage.

- Don't say yes without confirmation from God. *Don't marry in mystery.*

- The voice of the people is the voice of God.

- Never put pressure on yourself to marry. There is time for everything, and your time will come.

- If unsure, do your best, and leave the rest to your God.

- You cannot please everyone, so it is very normal for you to upset others even in your happy moment. This is because they will no longer have you to themselves in terms of time and sacrifices you make for them. As time goes on, they will then accept that you are no longer the little boy or girl they knew.

- Be prepared spiritually, psychologically, physically, and financially to be in a constant, continuous, self-sacrificing relationship and marriage forever.

- Make communication your best stool and forgiveness your daily bread.

On the Wedding Day

- Allow your family to be involved in your preparations. The more they are into your ceremony, the more it shows how generally they are happy for you and wish you a good union.

- Both people in the couple should be happy in and about the ceremony. Marriage is 100 per cent about happiness for both of you, and one shouldn't allow anything to get in the way of the ceremony at any time. *The happiness of your spouse should be your priority at all times.*

- Plan to spend what you can afford—less on your ceremony if you have less or more if you have more.

- There will be real and true hunger (dryness) in the marriage after your wedding if you don't spend money on the day very wisely.

After the Wedding Ceremony

- Be yourself after the wedding, be it a custom marriage or a white wedding.

- A wedding is a ceremony towards a long-lasting relationship known as a marriage. The relationship between you two must be continuous and better after the ceremony, so as to erase every doubt of your choice of partner.

- Be sure to talk about your future plans before the ceremony and also continuously work towards your plans in the marriage.

- Both partners should share funding towards the ceremony, as both so desire to be together. Marriages last when both people in the couple have planned and agreed to all their billings and are happy to share the joy of every profit they make together afterwards.

Staying Married

- Prior to marriage, have a clear reason for the union. Know deep in your heart why you want to be with this only person of among about seven billion people in the world.

- God thought marriage was for companionship and procreation—procreation in terms of not only having children but also having both partners develop and achieve their dreams in marriage.

- Marry someone whom you trust to clearly share your dreams and vision of your future with and who is happy to think with you on the same level.

- You can't marry or partner with anyone you can't trust to share his or her vision with you before marriage.

Wrong Reasons to Marry

- For merits (for example, if your partner has supported you through school or a project and, although uncertain about if he or she is right for you, you go ahead and marry him or her)

- For financial gain or financial interest through an arranged marriage

- For social status

There are many other wrong reasons to marry, such as for companionship only, for sexual legitimacy, or to make your fairy-tale-wedding dreams come true.

Adam told Eve about God's instruction in the Garden of Eden. You have responsibility for choosing your life partner, and you must choose wisely.

"Adam knew Eve as his wife" (Genesis 4:1 AMP). Amen.

Food for Thought

- Know the partner you choose. Know and cherish each other's interests and life plans and goals, and turn them into each other's determination to see both of you succeed and fulfilled in life.

- Don't enter marriage wanting to fix or change your partner. Only God can change the heart of a man or woman. In the story of the Israelites, God hardened the heart of the Pharaoh. In other texts of the Bible, God said He would soften the hearts of kings.

- Decide wisely whom you choose for a life partner. Your happy and fulfilled future depends on your choice.

- Analyse and evaluate your marriage daily, weekly, fortnightly, and so on.

- Don't sleep on any issue. Be bold enough to talk and share ideas that would help you and your partner's marriage and relationship become better. Be bold to take a walk if you have hit a bump and it's not working.

- Free yourself, for there is happiness beyond your relationship struggles.

Love yourself! Be yourself! Soar higher!

REFERENCES

"Broken Mirror Superstition." *Psychic Library*. http://psychiclibrary.com/beyondBooks/broken-mirror-superstition.

Elwell, Walter A. 1996. *Evangelical Dictionary of Theology*. Grand Rapids, MI: Baker Books.

"Marriage." *Wikipedia*, April 20, 2018. https://en.wikipedia.org/wiki/Marriage.

The Amplified Bible

New International Version Bible

ABOUT THE AUTHOR

Jenny A. Rogers is the founder of The Renewed Network, whose mission is to reach, teach, and inspire others through relationship coaching and speaking. Following a short-lived marriage and abandonment, she decided to pursue her long-desired passion to become a counsellor, and she is now a certified Listener in the UK. She has now renewed her thoughts and attitudes towards relationship building and has helped many people achieve this as well. Jenny is determined to help many more make right choices in marriage and all forms of relationships.